2022 by Chris Bruce
TheInternetLandlordBook.com

All rights reserved. No part of this book may be used, reproduced, or transmitted in any form or by any means, electronic or mechanical, including photocopying and recording, or by any information storage or retrieval system, without permission from the publisher, except by a receiver who wishes to quote brief excerpts in connection with a review in a newspaper, magazine, or electronic publication.

www.TheInternetLandlord.com

chris@theinternetlandlord.com

Dedication

I want to start by first dedicating this book to every single entrepreneur out there that has been on the struggle bus of trying to get their business from an idea to actually in fruition making money, and thriving. Listen, I was, once you I had a very big vision of where I saw myself and my business going not too long ago. And I remember saying to myself, when I do make it, my whole goal in life will be to give back and help someone like myself to get there much faster.

I want to shout out to all my mentors along the way, all the books that I've read. And the reason I've created this book specifically for you is to help you to be able to get through the learning curve much faster than it took me. Listen, if you read this book in its entirety, I promise you, the things that you're going to learn and discover will ultimately make a big shift in your mind. If you take action on information, it will catapult you to the success that you're looking for.

Whether that's making 6 or 7 figures a year in your business or making 6 or 7 figures in a month in your business, it can do for you what it has done for me and many others that I've trained. I've spent the last 10+ years educating people in the real estate space. I've had a lot of people ask me, Chris, teach us how you are generating income from online. So, that is the reason, why I've created this Internet Landlord book.

It's the name of my company, the name of my investments. I am here today to show you guys how you can become an internet landlord and use the internet to cash flow and literally make tons of money, but also leave a legacy by transforming the lives of your customers and your clients. So, I hope this book serves as inspiration and illumination for you that fills you up with energy, fills your mind up with ideas. So, that way you can go out and have the change that you want in your business, and literally make the change in the world, by implementing everything that you're going to read from here.

So, I challenge you. Never give up on your dream. Do not share any of your big ideas with small-minded people. Go out there and execute your ideas and everything that you want in life will come true.

Table of Contents

Table of Contents ---------------------------*5*

Introduction ---------------------------------*1*

Freedom Isn't Cheap, in Fact Its Quite Expensive -------------------------------------*7*

Residential Landlord Vs Internet Landlord-15

Brick & Mortar to Click & Order ----------*27*

CAN ANYONE BECOME AN INTERNET LANDLORD? --------------------------------*41*

Why Me? ------------------------------------*45*

Before You Make a Course, You Need This 56

Creating Your Intellectual Property ------*66*

HOW TO TEACH ---------------------------*75*

What McDonald's Taught Me About Selling Courses For Maximum Profit --------------*84*

Why Leaving Digital Footprints Will Build Trust And Your Bank Account ------------*96*

How To Print Money From Emails -------*112*

Get Them Off The Fence -----------------*125*

You Have An Obligation To Become Rich -- 132

Introduction

Internet Landlord. That's actually a term that I coined back in two thousand eleven (2011). It's actually what I also named my company after. I came up with this name because it was basically saying how to turn your intellectual property into a cash flowing asset. Meaning taking the knowledge and expertise that you have and putting it in some type of online program, course, mentorship, or software that other people can use and learn from. You end up benefitting from selling that course and cash flowing off of that information.

And so, I saw this early on, happening from a mentor of mine back around 2010. This was when I first got started in real estate. I saw a bunch of quotes and unquote gurus selling information and at the time, I just wanted to learn how to make money. So, for me, I really didn't look at how much money they were making nor did I really care.

All I cared about was to learn and soak up the game of how I can get started in real estate investing, finding a different way to make money on the side. That's exactly what I did. I invested in programs, to catapult me into my first business which was real estate wholesaling bank-owned properties. Now, what took me down a rabbit hole, I never thought would happen in a million years. Never set out to even know anything about making money online. But what happened in a short period of time shifted and changed my entire life. And in this book, I want to be able to do that for you as well.

So, I'll never forget fast forward. 2010, it was a hot sunny day. About 85-degrees out and a guy by the name of Preston Ely, was sitting in Starbucks. So, I walked in to get my protein shake. I'm not a coffee guy, so I'd always walk in there to get a protein shake set up and open my computer to do some work. Now, typically, when I would walk into Preston, I would say, what's up to him, keep it moving. He would only be in there for about 10 to 15 minutes and then he would leave and I wouldn't see him again.

But this time, he stayed in there for a little bit over 45 minutes. And so quietly, I just sat in my chair with my computer, and every few minutes I would just look over. Sometimes, I would see him get excited, sometimes I would see him very focused. I remember at 12:00 PM it was getting ready to go from 11:59 to 12:00 PM, and I later found out that he was getting ready to launch his very own software.

When it was launched, I remember getting the notification on my phone from the email that this software was live. The software he launched was not cheap software at all, actually, it cost about $3,000 to invest. He went ahead and launched it. I literally saw him press a button while in Starbucks and bring in over a million dollars in less than 15 minutes. That is when a light bulb went off in my head and said, wow, this is amazing.

I have been wanting to make a million dollars in real estate and I literally saw this guy press a button and make a million dollars in 15 minutes. And I could not believe it, but it inspired me.

I was born and raised in Detroit, Michigan. The thoughts of making a million dollars were very farfetched. I do come from a lower middle-class type of home. You see, my mom was a hard-working mom. We had a stepfather in the house. He really didn't make much money. My dad and mom did whatever they can to make ends meet. She made about $1,200 a month raised three kids. Even though my dad and her weren't together. I still got the best of both worlds because growing up, my dad always had his own business as well as worked for the Ford Motor Company.

So, he made pretty good money back in the 90s, 6 figures which probably today would be worth somewhere close to high 6 or low 7 figures. So, he was doing really well for himself. But one thing about it was he worked his butt off. I'm talking about I rarely saw my dad unless I was helping in his tax business. And so, I got to see how hard it was for him to make those 6 figures a year that he was making. It was non-stop hours of work after work, and so I was taught that for you to make a lot of money, you need to work a lot of hours daily. And that was a myth and something that I had accepted for years.

It's kind of the reason why at the age of 19, I was pushing three jobs because I had a feeling that this was going to be how I will make a ton of money. Boy, was I wrong? Going back to think about when I saw this guy, Preston, literally press a button for 15 minutes of work to make such an amount of money. And don't get me wrong, I'm pretty sure it was more hours put into creating the software including back and forth meetings with developers and things like that. But to see that there weren't any hard manual labor hours that he did, intrigue me.

He pressed the button and made money, and not just a little amount of money but he made million dollars within a short period. It literally had my eyebrows raised to the sky and I had to learn more. That was my journey of figuring out how I will later on, become an Internet Landlord.

Freedom Isn't Cheap, in Fact Its Quite Expensive

In 2009, I find myself getting ready to be at a crossroad. I was trying to figure out what I was going to do now that I had brought a little girl (my daughter) into the world. I was working at Bank of America, processing loans, doing data entry work for $12 an hour. Now, if you do the math, I was bringing home $1,500 before taxes. The issue was that after I paid rent, car notes, insurance, and food for the baby, I barely had anything left over.

So, I did as most people did. I would go on the internet and search for side hustles, other little schemes, and ways to make money. I would invest in some of them and enjoy some of the free ones but I would never end up making any money. I even tried the MLMs. I joined some of the top network marketing programs. But after begging my friends and family to get into it and they rejected my proposal, I decided to give up.

It wasn't until I came across an advertisement on how to flip houses without using any cash or credit. Because I was able to invest in this program, and after making a bunch of mistakes, I found out that I had a passion for real estate. This real estate business allowed me to quit my job. Some of the lessons that I learned from my earl mentor were more than how to just make money. It was more on the paradigm shift that I needed to have in order to be a successful entrepreneur.

And I found myself getting to a point where I was finally able to bring enough revenue in from something outside of my job, and felt comfortable enough that it was time to quit my job. I actually blame it on reading Rich Dad Poor Dad, which was a recommended book that he told me that I need to read. So, if you're reading this, if you have already read Rich Dad Poor Dad, be careful. If you haven't again be careful. Because after reading the book, I decided to quit my job on May 7th, 2010.

When I quit my job, I didn't have a lot of savings but I was confident that I was going to be able to make money through my real estate business. Now, the thing about it was that when I quit my job, I felt free. I felt the freedom of now being able to control my own time. Being able to do what I want when I want. The only thing that I was missing was the actual money. And I struggled for weeks and months. Some deals that I had going on that were supposed to close fell through. And I found myself, unfortunately going through a breakup with my daughter's mom. I didn't have the finances to be able to take care of my daughter and I ended up back on my mom's couch trying to figure things out.

Fast forward, I even lost my car (repossessed) because I couldn't keep up with the note and the insurance. But one of the things that I learned was how to persevere, how to continue pushing and fighting through. Which ultimately led me to finally get momentum in my business and make money. The thing about entrepreneurship is that we see the glitz and glamour that we think is going to come with it as soon as you are an entrepreneur. And all we can think about is the freedom that we're finally going to have. But I'm here to tell you that freedom is expensive. Oh yeah, it comes with a cost. A cost of late nights. A cost of not being able to take vacations with your friends on holidays like Memorial Day on the 4th of July. A cost of sacrificing time spent with your kids or even your loved ones.

That cost can be very expensive and sometimes it can even become detrimental to your health. But that burning desire in your body is what will keep you going through the midst of all of the chaos, trials, or tribulations that you may go through with building your business. Is building a business very easy? Not at all. That's why everybody does not become successful in building one or keeping one. But I can tell you that it's very simple.

You see, in my real estate business, I found myself not having as much freedom as I thought. I really had an overpaid job, because I had to go out there and produce over and over and over again and I found myself chasing checks. Even though some of the checks were big and I would make pretty good money off of them, I would still have to continue right after chasing another check and it was very much a lot of my time. You see, entrepreneurs will quit working 40 hours a week to end up working anywhere from 18-20 hours a day on their business. And in the beginning, sometimes that is needed. It's needed for you to be able to hit those goals and those aspirations that you have. But eventually, you will get burned out.

Eventually, you will get to a point where your health will deteriorate. Eventually, your loved ones will be upset with you, because you will miss months or maybe even years from some of the most memorable times when you should be there. And so, what I did was I made a pivot. Since I was really good at real estate and I had tons and tons of people asking me how they could get into the business. I found my lane and which is my passion right now. Which is teaching others how to do what it is that I've been able to accomplish. And that is what I want you to think about.

You see, being able to create the ultimate freedom business is not just making a lot of money but also having a lot of your time. And that is the reason why an internet landlord when you become one, you're able to create tons and tons of passive income without having to work tons and tons of hours. There are a lot of different things in the business that can be automated and the rest can be delegated.

Now, I find myself only working about 3 to 4 hours a week. That's because I have a pretty solid team and I have a lot of things automated as well too. Will you get there in the first 30 days? No, But you can get there within the first 12 months or even 24 months. And that is why I tell people when you think about what it is that you want. Figure out what is your income goal and figure out what is your time goal? How much time would you like to buy back? How much more time would you like to spend with your loved ones? Maybe taking vacations. Maybe investing or doing some other things that you're passionate about that has nothing to do with making money.

You see, I know a lot of multimillionaires that don't have much time. They also are not that happy and even though we believe that money is ultimately the thing that will make us happy, it's not. It's freedom. So, this is why I'm so passionate now and showing others how to go out and turn their knowledge, their expertise into an online business. Because I know it can break you through the hours of slaving away from whatever business or things that you have going on. Maybe, you have a career or job that you're working in and you have this fire, this burning passion that's inside of you that you know you could be teaching and helping others at something that you're really good at, but you just don't know where to start. Or maybe you're scared.

Maybe, you're afraid to get on the other side of your comfort zone. Because you don't believe that anybody would actually even pay you for that information and knowledge. But I'm here to tell you that they will. And I'm here to tell you that every single day that you let go by without being able to get this information out. You really just cutting off years, months, days, of your life and time to get your freedom back.

The faster you get to your dream life the longer you'll be able to enjoy it. And that is why it is time now for you to go out and become an internet landlord and start to teach others that thing that you're absolutely good or even great at.

Residential Landlord Vs Internet Landlord

Residential landlord versus internet landlord. I came from a background in real estate investing. I want to take you back to 2006. I was turning 21 at the time. I was actually twenty getting ready to turn 21. This was around April, and I never forget when I got the call from my dad. I just moved to Florida a year prior. I got a call from my dad who was living in Jamaica, who had told me that there was a huge opportunity for me to become a landlord, a homeowner. Never in a million years did I ever thought I would own a property at 20. But at this time this was when the real estate market was on fire.

It was actually during the housing bubble that later on was getting ready to completely crash and change the lives of almost every American across America, right. So, I got this call that I could get this house in Detroit. I'll never forget. It was actually a duplex on the east-side of Detroit, Michigan. I'd never been on that side of town before. And I was excited because being a homeowner even though it was not on my list, I was enticed that I was actually going to be able to make money upfront as a landlord.

This was during the subprime loan crisis where people were getting loans left and right for houses, taking money out of equity to put in their pocket. Now, I would say that that's necessarily not really legal and I wouldn't tell anybody to do that. The only reason I'm telling you this is because we're past the statute of limitations. But it's something that I had no clue what I was getting myself into, but I was excited to become a landlord. And so, what happened was I trusted my dad, trusted what they were telling me that I was going to be able to do. I made a little bit of money upfront about $9,000 and I could tell you that I felt rich.

$9,000 at 20 years old and a new homeowner. I couldn't believe I even got approved for a loan. Because I was working at the time for a company that was in partnership with a cold-calling company that was working for General Motors. Helping customers that were having a problem with their vehicles. And so, the thing about it was that I could not believe that at the age of 20, I'm a homeowner. I got about $9,000 in my pocket. And now, I have to service and find a tenant for this property because I'm in Florida. I'm not going to be able to keep up with you know the rent payments and things like that.

So ended up coming across a friend of mine Roland. I actually worked with him at a prior job back in Detroit for the Tigers at Comerica Park selling cotton candy & lemonade. I ended up talking to him. He needed a place to stay. So, he went ahead and I set it up for him to become my tenant. I felt relieved that I got money that's going to be getting paid into the mortgage. I had a little money upfront I had to play with. So, I was good.

Now back then, I had no money management skills and I completely blew through that money in about 6 months. Going out partying doing all types of stuff. Wasting money on alcohol bottles and just clothes and stuff that meant nothing. But to me, it meant everything at the age of 20. Then the bad news came. Unfortunately, my tenant which I didn't know at the time was doing some other illegal activities that ended up getting him murdered. And now I have this property that I have to take care of and pay the mortgage on every single month, and I'm no longer bringing in any additional cash flow.

So, I literally went from the American dream of having a home and actually even making money from it to now it's become my nightmare. Because not only did my friend end up dying, but now I have a house that is in Detroit vacant, and I am thousands of miles away, and not able to manage it. So, unfortunately about 6 months later, I ended up not being able to keep up with the mortgage payments. And I lost that house to foreclosure. Now, remember this was around the time in 2007 when the whole housing market was coming to a crash anyway. Almost everybody was losing their property. And we literally had seen a complete crumble of the housing market all across America.

So, at this time, it put a real big nasty taste in my mouth when it came to being a landlord. I grew up knowing that one of the fastest ways to grow wealth was owning properties. But what they didn't tell me was the challenges and things that you had to deal with when tenants aren't able to pay. I wasn't able to find another tenant for the property and I couldn't keep up with it and I had no idea what I was doing. So, unfortunately, I lost the property.

Now, fast forward about 4 or 5 years later and I saw people making money online. And the thing about it was that there were people that were educating others about the knowledge and information that they already were doing or applying in their own business. They were creating little single-family houses in a sense businesses, or I should say assets where they were able to cash flow like a landlord. They would take a book and would turn it into like a digital book, where it was online, easily downloadable. And this asset which was an intellectual asset. The information they took out of their brain and put into a form of a book. They would sell it which would then create cash flow every single month.

Then I would see some of them would turn another intellectual asset into a digital course. They would take their information to create videos and workbooks and worksheets and then put that into a membership site. Where members would have to pay a monthly fee just like a tenant in order to access the information. I saw someone that had a subscription-based intellectual asset that they were charging around $97 a month. Now, they had 3,000 people paying them $97 a month.

So, I want you to do the math on that, okay. 3,000 people times $97 that was about $291,000 that they were making on a monthly basis. So, when you start to look at an Internet Landlord right. Someone that owns an intellectual asset like a course, or an eBook, they are able to scale to a higher amount of revenue coming in without having a huge overhead like a traditional landlord.

So, for me, as things start to shift, fast forward now we're in the year 2022 as I'm writing this book, becoming an Internet Landlord makes more sense overall than being a traditional landlord when it comes to scaling.

Now, I'm not speaking against the building of wealth far as asset protection when it comes to owning properties and becoming a residential landlord, but let's just be honest. Managing a hundred properties with a hundred different tenants trying to make sure that they pay rent on the first, is 100 times a lot more work than managing 100 customers paying $97 a month. The subscriptions and management of the payments can be done specifically online. You can set automation to remind them of payments and even when a payment fails, again there could be automation or you can have someone that could contact them to make sure they get the payment. Or even if they want to unsubscribe, it's not a problem. And this is why I tell people, that the fastest way to build wealth in today's age is becoming an internet landlord. And the fastest way wealth is by becoming a residential be even a commercial landlord.

, you can take your intellectual property. Create them into courses, eBooks, memberships, masterminds, and mentorship programs. Produce a large amount of wealth and then be able to take that money and dump that into real estate where now you're protected asset-wise when it comes to taxes. Because as you start to make more money, you will need to offset the income that you're making with tax write-offs. So, assets like having residential properties or commercial properties. But when it comes to being able to make money fast, you're going to be able to do that by becoming an internet landlord creating cash flow online.

I don't believe in the whole issue with people saying, oh, get rich quick schemes. Here's the thing. You know when you look at it when it comes to the whole get rich quick. Well, who wants to actually get rich slowly? Right? And so, when people say this, I'm like I understand but no one wants to take 5, 10 years to get rich. When you think about the scheme, the word scheme itself is schematic, right. Schematic is the plan or blueprint. So, we've been warned all of our lives that get-rich-quick schemes should stay away from. And to me, I say yes be aware of getting rich quick schemes. But in all reality, we all want to be into a get rich quick scheme. Because if we have the plan or blueprint to get rich quickly, why wouldn't we go ahead and do that?

You see, wealth today is measured in time more than money, right. Because acquiring money it's very simple. If you provide a service or benefit, someone in exchange will give you money for that. But I want you to think about this. If you were to make a million dollars in let's say 10 years. And most people don't make that in 10 years. Honestly, most people probably make that over a 30, 40-year mark. So, let's just go with real math. 40 years that takes you to make a million dollars in your lifetime, would you say that that person is rich? No.

But if that person can go out and create something, something of high value where they sell that transformation to their customers or their clients and make a million dollars in a year, or make a million dollars in 6 months, or maybe even in one month. Would you then consider that they're rich? Yes. The answer would be yes, they are. That's why I say that it's easier to make a lot of money in a short period of time than it is to make a little money in a long period of time.

You see, if you take 30, 40 years to make a million dollars. That's just too long to build wealth. Especially when you have knowledge that can literally turn into a digital asset that can be shared with the world and change the lives of hundreds of thousands of people. You're able to create wealth a lot much faster. I want you to think about how much it costs to even acquire real estate nowadays, right? At the time of writing this book, the real estate market is completely on fire post-pandemic. We are seeing interest rates at an all-time low but house pricing at an all-time high.

So, in order to even create a $10,000 a month business being a landlord unless you're getting duplexes, triplexes, or even commercial buildings.

If you're just getting single-family rental properties, you're going to have to spend millions of dollars in capital to be able to acquire enough single-family houses that will produce that type of cash flow on a monthly basis. Yet becoming an Internet Landlord, creating an online business, you can literally start with just a few hundred dollars.

You may have to invest more if you want to create a funnel and have someone do a lot of sales copywriting for you. It might cost you a few thousand dollars if you want that whole service done for you. But in order to even get someone to spend money with you, you need to be willing to invest in yourself. Let's take, for instance, you have a consulting mentorship business. Without building a website, without building a funnel, you could go out there and just use the audience you already have. You can just put a message out there for people interested in getting your services or mentorship from you to DM you or message you. You can create the first client's customer base just by doing that without any website at all. And that is why I like the internet and that is why I believe a Internet Landlord is the fastest way to create wealth in today's market and today's time.

Brick & Mortar to Click & Order

Now, I may be showing my age a little bit with this one. But I remember the days of having to go into the library or going to Barnes and Noble for your favorite book. I enjoyed those times having a library card and being able to go in there and kick it with my friends from middle school, and high school. Nowadays, you can literally click a button from your phone, tablet, or computer and have the book, sometimes even on the same day deliver straight to your doorstep.

I remember the times of having, for instance, to do taxes and walking into a tax business figuring out exactly what the government, owed you for all of the money that you have worked, paid out for that whole calendar year. Once again, nowadays, you can literally go on a computer, put in your info, crunch some numbers, and you'll know exactly how much your return is and you'll get that wired directly into your account in two or three weeks. We have gone from brick-and-mortar to to click and order. And I will say being able to go through the global pandemic which we've gone through in 2020.

It really took it to the next level of that. While we see so many businesses that have gone down unfortunately because of the pandemic, a lot of those brick-and-mortar stores weren't able to survive. And other businesses we saw thrived including mine during the pandemic. And many of those businesses that did thrive were online businesses. Once again, we went from being able to have to go into your favorite restaurant to get your favorite food, and having that whole experience, to now you can click a button on your phone and have food delivered straight to your doorstep in 20 minutes or less.

We've gone ladies and gentlemen into the new age of the internet. We went from internet 1.0 to 2.0 to now we're actually even moving into the next phase with the metaverse and things of that nature. So, I say all this to let you know that the internet is not going anywhere and for some of you that may be a little bit older and you're not as well versed with social media and the internet. Well, it's time to put those excuses behind you and get involved. For those of you that are a little bit younger and grew up with nothing but the internet, you're in the right space. You're in the right time and it's time to be able to take that knowledge or expertise that you have and turn that into a business where someone can click and order your services, your products, your programs, and be able to duplicate a level of some of your success for themselves all right.

So when we talk about intellectual property, I want you to think about what is something that comes easy to you but harder to others. This could be something far as maybe you're good in fitness and you have a specific workout that you do on top of the diet that you continue being disciplined on and it's got you results. It's gotten you to the goal weight that you've wanted. Maybe, you're a person that is good at helping struggling couples in relationships and you've been able to apply this to your own relationship. You've maybe even helped some of your friends or family members rekindle their relationship. And you can come out with a program to help others get through troubling times and get through those struggling moments in times when a couple is almost ready to end it and break up.

Maybe, you're someone that is good when it comes to financial literacy and you're good at making other people money. Maybe, this can be in a form of real estate which is where I've come from, my background. Maybe you're good in a crypto or the NFT space. Maybe, you're good in stocks. It doesn't really matter specifically what it is but whatever your zone of genius, whatever something that comes very easy to you and harder for others, it is time to think about how you can take that intellectual property, create books, eBooks, courses, right. Mentorship programs and turn that into an online business for you.

I want to talk about the mindset of an internet landlord. Because in order to have a business where you can make hundreds of thousands and even millions of dollars, you first have to adopt the mindset. One of the big things about internet landlords is the power of investing into yourself.

You see before you go out and charge other people money, you have to understand that what you do not know will hurt you. What you don't know will affect you from getting to the next level and the fastest way to be able to make tons of money is paying directly for that information yourself as well. As internet landlords, we believe in taking the shortest route to get to success by paying others for their expertise and knowledge which will then allow us to go out and charge others for our expertise and knowledge.

For years; I did what most of you probably have done before. I went out search YouTube typed in how to make money online, and went on following every single guru, getting on their email list for the freebies that they might have given away. Searching for all these different tips and tricks and free training here and free seminars there and gaining tons and tons of information, but really becoming more and more confused. Someone that pays — pays attention. Even though some of the information that you may see that is free can be good, until you invest in other people's programs, then you will start to see that you will attract people to pay for yours as well.

For years I was stuck around 150,000 a year, right. I didn't really take this online seriously until about 2013. Back then I was making about $5,000 a month from my online business. At the end of 2013 literally the last month of the year; I invested my last at the time $2,000 because I was struggling. I invested $2,000 into this program called The Machine. It was set up as a course but it was also monthly calls which would allow me to get the information that I needed to set up where I could sell things and have everything automated where it would be running like a machine.

I'm talking about automated emails, having the funnel built out, everything that would make it run. I remember implementing everything and it was around March when things start to pick up for me. I don't know if you know March living in Florida, but in Florida, it's already 80-degree weather around that time. I remember going to the beach for a party, and my phone just kept notifying me, ringing repeatedly. It was these notifications that I was getting that notified me that people were consistently buying my eBook. Then upgrading to the course, then upgrade to my other upsell which was another course. And it was an amazing feeling just seeing my notifications going off back and forth and back and forth with people that were buying my programs.

I finally had built a well-oiled machine that end up getting me to the 10,000 - 13,000 a month consistently. Fast forward two years later, I said that it was time for me to invest in something else. It's time for me to find a new mentor. And I never forget coming across a Facebook post, not even sure how I ended up on this guy's friend list. But there was this guy by the name of Mitch who was offering for you to come live with him in a huge 8-bedroom mansion in Thailand. Now, I'd always dreamt of going to Thailand either for visiting or on vacation. Honestly, if you would ask me would I be able to live there for a whole month and be able to study with other internet landlords and entrepreneurs. Never in a million years, would I have thought that would happen.

And I was very nervous. Because to think of that, I'll have to be away from my girlfriend. Be away from my daughter, my family for 30 days in another country, on the other side of the world. I was afraid. But the one thing I learned about fear is, fear is false evidence appearing real or forgetting everything and running. So, I decided after talking with my girlfriend at the time and discussing with my family that it was best that I went ahead and took the leap of faith. I invested the $4,000 that it cost to go over there and learn from someone that had a skill that I very much needed. A skill that I would need as an internet landlord is copywriting.

Now, copywriting, if you don't know, is basically being able to put words on a page, a website that will transform your prospect into a client or customer, by the way of sales persuasion.

You see, it's not enough to say, hey, here's my course that's going to teach you how to invest in stocks and make you 10,000 a month, that's not going to get your prospect to become a customer. It's not enough to say, hey, I got a secret. I'm going to show you how to lose 10 pounds in the next 25-days using my diet. That's not enough.

You have to convince someone. You have to show someone the problem and you have to clearly show them that the solution to their problem is when they invest in themselves and buy your program or course. This is done by copywriting. These are the words that are printed on a page that acts as a 24-hour salesperson. So, copywriting is a top skill that every internet landlord must have to enable their online business to grow.

It was my pleasure to be able to work with one of the good copywriters that were responsible for writing tons of offers that have made multi-millions of dollars. So, I took that leap of faith, I flew into New York which was my layover. I went from New York and took an 18-hour flight to

Thailand. On my way there I was just thinking about all of the things that were going to happen. I was nervous. I didn't know any of the people there, it was kind of like that real-world TV show if you guys remember where you would just live with other people for several weeks. And I didn't know if there would just be drama. I was going to be the only black guy there. So I had no idea what to expect. But I can tell you still to this day it was one of the best investments that I ever made in my entire life.

Not only did I get a chance to live in a different country for a whole 30 days and adapt to their culture, but I also got to really learn the skill set of what it takes to turn someone from a stranger into a buyer and get your products and services. Which isn't an easy thing. I want you to remember, as an internet landlord, we typically do not meet our clients or customers ever in person. These people are entrusting you that your product or your service is going to transform their problem now to be solved. This could be a relationship problem. This could be a weight loss problem. This could be a financial problem. This could be a problem with parenting. There are all different niches that you can go into and the sky is the limit.

I literally saw people sell almost anything when it comes to online courses. The thing that you want to remember is it's all about transformation. So, as long as you're transforming someone from A to Z, you can get paid for it. So, I learned this copywriting skill and I learned also how to create value in the offer which would then allow me to be able to get paid. As a matter of fact, the guy that I was working with, Mitch who hosted this mastermind, helped me write one of my sales pages and offers. I made 6 figures in the course in less than 12 months and I still currently sell it today.

Now, what an internet landlord must understand is that this is not like working a job where you get paid for hourly work, as an internet landlord you get paid for how much value you bring to the marketplace in that hour and that is really the difference. So, going and looking back on that trip, I was able to take my income from making close to $140,000 to making over

$350,000 that following year. It was amazing and so I could definitely say the success of that trip was well worth it and if I could redo again, I would.

After a couple of years later, I figured it was time for me to invest in something else but this time, it was time to take it up a notch. Remember the greatest investment that you can make, the greatest bet that'll win every single time over putting money in the casinos or stocks is investing in yourself. I found myself in Orlando, Florida at a seminar called the Ask Method Live, and at this conference, there were about 500 people in the room. I was there for a 3-day seminar about different methods to again turn clients, prospects, into clients and customers. Through a certain methodology that this guy Ryan Levesque was teaching.

So, he made an offer but this time it wasn't $2,000. It wasn't $4,000. It was the biggest investment I had ever made in myself at the time. And that investment was $15,000 to work with this person and their team for one year. Now, I'll be honest with you. That $15,000 at the time was a big investment for me. I was nervous. The good thing is, I did have the support of my people that I had around me, my family, and they entrusted I was making the right decision on investing this $15,000 into this mentorship program.

Now, doing that not only did I quadruple my revenue, but I was also able to put systems and learn about team building, and put certain people into my company that still work for me today. I was able to really expand my business and think of it really like a real company. You see, before, it was me two virtual assistants and a salesperson. Working with this mentorship program, I expanded my team to four virtual assistants, two salespeople, and a project manager. Which was very key to helping me scale where I did close to a million dollars in revenue that following year. And see, this is the importance of investing in yourself and betting on yourself.

So, I can say that for me the people around me were very honest and very supportive of my investing in my education. Sometimes, you may not have that support. Sometimes, you may have family members or friends that are going to doubt you and tell you don't invest in yourself. But that is not the internet landlord way. In order for us to get people to pay us, we have to be willing to invest in ourselves in paying others to get that knowledge information that we do not have.

So, I tell you, don't share your big dream with small-minded people. Just go out there, invest in yourself, execute the things that you learn, and all of the dreams and aspirations that you have will come true.

CAN ANYONE BECOME AN INTERNET LANDLORD?

Can anyone become an internet landlord? The short answer is yes. You may be wondering or considering that you haven't had a lot of experience, or you may have not had the credentials of being in different magazines, or being on a big podcast and that's okay. Yes do those things help your credibility? Absolutely. I'm not gonna sit here and lie and say they don't, but to think about it, you don't have to be coin quote, unquote expert by some public opinion, because the truth is when you look at some of the biggest people in the world, people like Robert Kiyosaki or Tony Robbins, they didn't get a certification to do what they do. They just started from the ground up helping people. And then they got to the level where they're at now. So, do you have to have that certification from somebody nope not at all.

As long as you make a promise that you are going to help someone with whatever problem that they have, that's the only thing that is required as an internet landlord selling an online course. Now, you may be promising someone that you're going to be able to help them get their first Airbnb, or at least giving them the details and blueprint on how to do it, whether they do it or not, it's really up to them. But as long as you give them everything they need like the blueprint and instructions, then you've done your part. Maybe, you're a person that teaches dog owners how to walk a dog effectively without getting into a lot of chaos with other pets. There might be a certain way you go about doing this. Once again as long as you give them the strategies and instructions on how to effectively do that based on what you have done with other dogs, then that is fine.

Okay. So I just want you to get into that mode of you making a promise. Don't leave anything out go the extra mile for your customer. You do that then you have done your part. Now here's the thing, maybe you're not the expert or the person that wants to give the advice, but you are connected with a lot of other people that will. You can still become an internet landlord by publishing with other people that are knowledgeable about a certain topic or niche. Here's a prime example, Tim Ferris, which you guys may or may not know. He has written the book the four-hour workweek. So he came out with a book tribe of mentors, and basically what he did was he recorded his conversations and interviews with tons of different people that he has worked with or came across.

He then used those recordings to go out and publish a book. If I'm not mistaken, this book actually went bestseller. He didn't rely strictly on his knowledge, but he went and got some other individuals that were good in their specific niche realm. Put those interviews together and was able to publish this book. You could do the same thing with an online course. You could interview some of the top people in their respect, business or niche, or topic, put that together into an online digital course and be able to sell that to the masses.

The exact strategy that my mentors, when I first got started in real estate did with their first program in 2009, I came across a course called the Reo Rockstar. And that rockstar which I told you about earlier became my mentor, but the guy that actually was the one who was doing all of the deals and providing the content in the course was a guy named Lee. These guys went on to make millions of dollars selling this course, which was a physical course at the time. And this is a prime example that you do not have to be the person with the knowledge. You just have to be able to get access to it, package it up, and then you can sell it and make a very, very big profit.

Why Me?

But why should I? I know that's the one thing that you're probably thinking. What makes me so special that I should create a course and become an Internet Landlord? How are people going to see value in me and feel like paying me hundreds or thousands of dollars for my knowledge or expertise? That's the one thing that I happen to see a lot with new up and coming Internet Landlords they get the imposter syndrome. They wonder how will I get someone to even see that I'm worth charging $500 or $1,000 or even $10,000 for the services.

You see, people are willing to pay for information and insight from somebody that they feel is a step above them. And many of you reading this book now, you're much more ahead of other people than you think.

You don't have to be in Forbes Magazine or have hundreds of thousands of followers just to get people to invest in your course, your program. Yeah, those things can help. But I would tell you before I had a big following before I got any type of articles, I was able to establish myself as a go-to real estate investor and mentor because I focused on documenting the process. For the women reading this book, the one thing that I would say is that you have an advantage over a lot of men today, and not saying all, but women like to get close to other women to build community. They get close to other women because they are vulnerable. And so, you don't have to even show that you have a perfect life or that you have it all figured out.

People like to be a part of tribes. They like to be around people that are keeping it real. And so, start to document your process. The good, the bad, the ugly. That will draw so many people to you. And that when it is time to launch your course or program. People will buy from you just because they like, they know, and now they trust you, and that is the key to making a lot of profit and cash flow as an Internet Landlord. The faster you can get people to like, know, and trust you is how you will get people to spend money with you.

Let's go into details about what that looks like. For many of you, I'm pretty sure you are on social media. That's probably how you even found out about me and this book. You can use whatever platform that you use the most. I tell people to go to where their audience is. The good thing about it is more than likely for most of you depending on what niche you're in, your audience is on most platforms. Even new social media platforms like TikTok have billions of people on there. You can't tell me that your audience isn't on there. Even though it's used for mostly dances and entertainment.

But you can use Facebook, you can get into Instagram which is one of my favorites, or even YouTube to go out there and start to document your process and talk to your audience. Talk to your prospect that would be an ideal customer for you. You would do this with a series of videos, you could show content of your life and your lifestyle. You can do videos of skits or funny videos to bring awareness to yourself and you brand. People love to be entertained and you can educate with it BOOM you will be able to grow a lot faster. The more you're able to show that you're human and show your personality, that is how you're going to draw people to you. And just keep in mind, most of the time that you are putting out content the things your ideal client is into is probably the same things you're into as well. More than likely, they're going to be very similar and have some of the same characteristics as you.

You're almost looking for you but maybe a little bit in a better form potentially. Not saying that you're bad or anything like that but just saying. That is who you're going to naturally attract to you. Maybe, you're an avid reader. You can talk about some of the books and things that you've read or you can even show how well you're versed in that niche or what you're going to be by doing some tutorials. That actually works really well on

YouTube or if you're on Instagram doing short reels or as well as TikTok.

Now, you don't have to be on every single social media platform. In fact, you could probably just focus on one or maybe two. We have this thing where you can repurpose your content and I tell every creator that is what you absolutely should be doing. What I mean by that is that you should be going out and if you have a video, you should be posting it on all the platforms that you're on. So, you can post it on TikTok, you post a video on Facebook and you can go ahead and post it on Instagram. This will get you a long way to reach and will help to get your message across to your ideal client.

Now another thing that is really big that works well is going live on Instagram. And yes, first if you don't have a big followers, you're not going to have that many people that would jump on. But who cares? You continue to do it. And what you can do to big up your followers or even big up the people that are watching your Instagram live is by simply collaborating with others. Now, most people would think, why would I want to collaborate with someone that is in the same niche as me or does the same thing as me? See internet landlords our mindset is collaboration over competition.

Listen, there are 7 billion people on this Earth, and the fact of the matter is, that just because you may be in the same niche, or have a similar offer as someone else doesn't mean that they're not going to spend money with you, or even that other person. A lot of times people will end up buying both of yours, plain and simple. I'll give you an example. Being a real estate educator for 10 + years now. I've had very good relationships with other real estate experts out there. And many times I've even had my customers tell me that they bought one of my friends' courses as well too. It's fine All right. It's not like they're going to just pick one person and not pick someone else or not buy someone else's support. So, that's why as an Internet Landlord, one of the things that we are big on is having an abundant mindset.

Now, I can go into mindset really deep into this book but I'm not going to go too deep right now, but I do want you to make sure that you do adopt an abundant mindset. There's no such thing as lack. There's no such thing that it's not enough because that is not true. And remember whatever you focus on expands. So, if you focus on the abundance of everything around you and the abundance of all of the customers and clients that are out there wanting to spend money with you, then that is what you will get.

Focus on figuring out what problem you will solve in the marketplace. Because at the end of the day, especially now in 2022 people don't care about how many years of experience you have. I can't tell you how many times I'm seeing a lot of educators that maybe have only been in business for a year but they've been able to get results for themselves. And they know how to also teach others and they're making millions of dollars doing it, and listen, there's nothing wrong with that. I know a lot of you will end up getting the imposter syndrome at some point, but I want to go ahead and make sure that you go and just give up that whole idea that you're an imposter.

If you are even just two or three steps ahead of somebody which again, many of you are. Because most of the people that you're going to probably be selling your product or course of mentorship to will be a lot of newbie people. They don't even know some of the terminology or contracts or certain different things, or methodologies that you happen to know. Now, I'm not recommending that if you've never even had the success for yourself that you should be coming out with the course a leadership program. No, not at all. But if you have been able to see some early success document your process.

And if you do find a way where you've made it, where you can continually, repeatedly get those results, now it's time for you to go out and help others get those results. Why not get paid for it? It's not a bad thing. Money is the exchange of value. So, if you have value to give to someone else, you damn sure should be getting paid for it.

Plus, one time my mentor had a good conversation with me and it took me a little bit of surprise because I was expecting to have a different conversation about business, but he was actually talking about me being selfish. The conversation was about me being on the fence at the time of coming out with a course. He was explaining to me that you are selfish if you do not come out with programs to help others. He said, once you actually get success with something and you end up having a process around it where you pretty much mastered it. It's time for you to go out there and also share with others.

He said you're doing the world a disservice if you are not sharing your gift with others. It also made me think about what people will know me for. You see when you think about it in long term is that most of the people that we still talk about today, your Martin Luther Kings, your Malcolm X's, your Biggie Smalls, Tupac's. I mean, you name it. They have a legacy that they created that now lives on past them. And yes, you could be really good at something, you can make a lot of money from something. But if you didn't help others what will your legacy be? What would somebody say at the eulogy at your funeral? Oh, this person made a bunch of money. No

They're going to remember how you made them feel. They're going to remember what you did for them. And that's what struck a nerve with me is that I wanted to make sure that I left my impact on the world, that when I do say and take my last breath that many people will celebrate what I did for them, how I made them feel and this is why becoming an internet landlord is bigger than just making money. Yes, the money is going to give you the lifestyle you want, it's going to give you the freedom that you want. But more importantly, it's going to give you the impact and legacy that will live on for generations and years to come.

So, whenever that imposter syndrome starts to kick in and you say to yourself, oh I don't know if I should create this course. I want you to stop. I want you to reread this chapter and immediately throw that thought out of your mind. No thought lives in your head rent-free. You will have to pay for every single thought, positive or negative. So, you might as well focus on the positive and not the negative. It's time to evict it. You need to make sure that your thoughts are in abundance and align with what you want in life because that is the Internet Landlord's way.

Before You Make a Course, You Need This

So, there's one thing you must have before you go out and create your eBook, digital course, or mentorship program. In fact, if you don't have this, it's literally the difference between making just a few thousand dollars to making hundreds of thousands or even millions of dollars, and I learned my lesson early on. When I created my first course in 2011 I literally just put it out there to the market, but when I did it was crickets.

I only sold to 6 people and I was wondering, why isn't my course selling? I'm showing proof that I'm closing deals. I've even helped other people that are my friends to close deals and I was being very transparent. But yet, no one was buying my course. I came across a guy, I can't remember his name, an Australian guy and he was talking about how to make your product or service unique. His video really sparked my mind, because he talked about these different unique messages that most companies had that I never even paid attention to.

We actually call this a unique selling proposition or USP and it's clear what makes your product to be unique from everybody else's. I want you to think about Domino's, right. Back in the day and you may not remember this, but their unique selling proposition was that you would get your pizza in 30 minutes or less or it's free. One of the favorite insurance company commercials that you always see, Geico. In 15 minutes, you could save 15% or more on your car insurance. These are unique selling propositions. It's what makes them unique from other insurance companies, other pizza restaurants that will make you say, I want to go ahead and order or I want to go ahead and buy from them instead of their competitors.

Also having a REI Wealth Academy name, there was no uniqueness in my product. So, this was clear why nobody was buying my product at all. I was just another quote-unquote guru trying to pitch his real estate program just like everybody else. So, I went to the lab. I started thinking, what could I create that would make my product different? What can make my products stand out? I thought about different names and I came up with Virtual Flipping Riches 3.0, which later on became Get That First Deal.

Now, the difference between this program from my older one was, I had a unique selling proposition. Because I was teaching people how to flip properties virtually without stepping foot inside the property, or seeing the seller or buyer. You, see?

This is not just to show you how to flip houses program. I'm showing you how to do this remotely and without even having to see the house. That's why my product was able to go out and sell millions of dollars. It won me my 2-Comma Club award in 2021 with Clickfunnels for hitting a million dollars in sales with that product alone. And that course was $997. So, before you create your course, your mentorship program, your eBook, I want you to think about, what can you make yours unique? What would be your unique selling proposition? It doesn't matter about the competition. It doesn't matter if other people are bigger than you in the marketplace.

Listen, there are 7 billion people on the Earth. That means that there's enough money and people to go around that will buy your product. And guess what? The cool thing about it is that a lot of times people will buy from multiple different people because they can learn different things from more than one person. I never heard a rapper say I'm not going to come out with a record because Jay Z or Lil Wayne came out with one. So that's the same mindset you have to have when you are becoming Internet Landlord and creating your product.

Now, with a unique selling proposition, you also need a unique mechanism. Now, what a unique mechanism is its how you're delivering on your promise of a unique selling proposition. So, for example, I was showing people how to do deals virtually again without stepping foot on their property, meeting sellers or buyers, and doing it from their computer or cellphone. How I delivered on that was my unique mechanism which I was showing them how to use our text messaging software to put deals together. Again, without having to necessarily meet the homeowners in person and being able to use the power of the internet to send out contracts and delegate certain tasks.

So, my unique mechanism just a kind of put it in context for you guys was the TACO method and so the TACO method was formed off of a story that I created. One day, it was taco Tuesday. I was eating my tacos with my friends. I end up getting a phone call from a number that was not stored in my phone. When I looked at the number, I didn't recognize it. So, I quickly put the phone down. A minute later I got a text message from that same exact number. It was a message from one of my old friends from high school. He had changed his number and told me to give him a call when I got this message. Now, it hit me.

There was a paradigm shift right there. The light bulb went off because I quickly realized that I would have never answered that phone call because it wasn't stored in my phone. However, I would answer a text message, and that is a fact with most people out in the world do today. They won't answer many phone calls that are not stored in their phone. However, they will answer a text message or at least look at it. And so, that's when it hit me that I need to start text messaging homeowners and it was the quickest way to get in contact with them to offer them our services to be able to pick their property up and be able to then wholesale to a buyer.

So, we came up with the taco method which stood for Text, Analyze, Call, Offer, TACO and that was my unique mechanism. Now, creating this, the reason why it worked so well, the reason was because people were begging to deep dive and learn this whole TACO method strategy. I had convinced them that the only way they could get access to that strategy and my software was if they invested in my program. And see, that is how you can corner the market where you come up with your own unique mechanism on how you're going to deliver on your unique selling proposition, and people will have to buy your course, your mentorship, or your eBook.

They have to buy your program because you can't Google your unique mechanism. They can't go find it anywhere else because you made it. These are the two things that will set you up for success, having a unique selling proposition ,and having a unique mechanism and then you combine them together. It also creates an amazing offer that people are going to beg you to buy your product or your service. The next thing you need is a grand-slam offer.

Many people get confused about thinking the offer is just the product, but that's far from the truth. In fact, all of the other things that are around your product is what will make your offer much stronger. If you go out there and just say you can get my digital course for $297. I mean, if you have a big following and have some people that are interested, yeah, you're going to sell a few of them. But it will never be able to scale out to audiences of people that have no idea who you are.

You see, the goal of Internet Landlord is not just being able to create many assets, but having that one or two assets that will allow you to get as many tenants AKA customers into your world, so that creates more cash flow for you, right. So, the thing about it is that in order to scale to the masses, you have to have an absolute grand slam offer.

So, what's in the offer and what things you can include? One thing that if you're selling business consulting or some type of business venture or something that has to do with making money. A lot of times that will include contracts. Having a contract that's either pre-written out of some of the different things that need to be in their stipulations that is a value. Again, having some type of worksheets or cheat sheets, these are valuable as well too. Having a quick start video can be a part of the offer which is also a value play. If you have any software or calculators, this can also be added on as a bonus.

Now, if you are thinking about throwing some type of event, adding a free ticket or two, is an added bonus that will bring a lot of value. In fact, what I do for a lot of my mentorship students is that they get to come to my mastermind for free, which is a huge add-on bonus for getting into our mentorship program at the $10K plus level. Many times, you want to have at least three to four bonuses you want to make them even more valuable than the actual online course. This is why when people see the cost of the course, they will be so sold on the bonuses that to them it's worth buying the course just to get the bonuses for free.

That's the reason why having live tickets to events, brings up the value tremendously. You can even consider having maybe a coaching call or multiple coaching calls that they can sit in and have access to. Or if you've done past training before, they can get access to those replays.

So, make sure that when you are creating your offer you include, what's going to be entailed in the course but also the bonuses and other different things that you can add on just to make that offer a grand slam offering. And that is how to be able to scale your course to the moon.

Creating Your Intellectual Property

So, let's talk about creating your intellectual property. Intellectual property is your asset that you create like a book, an eBook. It can be a digital online course, or even if you have software. Now, this also can be later on turned into a mentorship or a mastermind. I want you to think about when it comes to creating your first intellectual asset, what would that be? Now, to establish authority, a lot of smart internet landlords will create a simple eBook. Now, this eBook will be about the topic that you are thinking about teaching.

Let's say, for instance, if you were wanting to teach how to leverage life insurance, you can create an eBook that explains a little bit of your journey but also gives strategies and tips. The reason why you create an eBook is that one, you can use it as a low-ticket offer to be able to convert people into a customer at a low cost. But also, it will establish authority because now, you're not just a quote-unquote guru, you're also an author. And everybody looks at authors very differently than the person that's just trying to sell their course or mentorship program.

Now, don't get me wrong. I've made a lot of money without having an eBook but I will say that life and business got a lot easier to sell when I did have one. So, if you don't have many followers or if you don't have an email list or text list and this is brand new to you, I will highly consider that you create an eBook. It's something that we actually do for our clients in addition to just establishing authority once again. So, when they're going to the marketplace, they have a low ticket offer that they can convert people and get to show people that they are experts that they do know what they're doing. And then, later on, they are upgrading them or what we call ascending them to the next product or service that they have. The eBook can range anywhere from free, $7 up to $37. Typically, when you do an eBook, you want to have some additional products for them to order while they're ordering. So, this can be in a form of if you turn your book into an audiobook. It can be a physical book. You can have a mini-course that you charge $37 to $47 or even $97 and these are things that you can add on as additional products which we call up sales to increase your average order value, right. So, after you have created your eBook, you can go out there and sell this to the masses but then you want to think about your next ascension product that you're going to get people to. So, for a lot of you like myself it will be your online digital course.

Now the thing about your online digital course which is great because once you create it, you can get paid over and over and over and over again. Now, when creating your digital course, you want to think about how I can get this person to have the transformation that they want. So again, let's just say, for instance, you're teaching somebody how to trade stocks. What you would do is you would start from the beginning far as the content that would be in the course. Maybe you start off with showing how to setup your account Understand how to read the signs and options. I'm not well versed in this niche but you get the idea.

You would literally map out from A to Z how you would get that person that transformation. Maybe it's a relationship niche that you're helping someone get through a breakup or strengthen the relationship. You want to literally think about it from the beginning to the end and you're going to break that down into five modules. Now, five modules, it can be four with a bonus module that's what makes it five. Inside those five modules, you will be able to create multiple videos.

It can also be audio too and you are going to want to create some checklist or workbooks or fast access, cheat sheets, PDFs basically to have things in written form that people can be able to look. Your niche or business that you may be promoting or for people to learn may require a contract, right. For me, after many years, I've taught people real estate investing, wholesaling, and they need a contract. So, I've included that and I've included training on how to fill that out. So, with the course, depending on your market, depending on your niche, you can market that and sell that anywhere from $97 all the way up to #2,000, and that's the great thing about it. It's a passive income asset that you can make money over and over and over again.

Now, selling digital courses, you can do typically about 1 to 2 million dollars in revenue. Sometimes, a little bit more but that's kind of where you usually typically cap out, especially, if your product is under $1,000. Now, the thing about it, and one of the things that I absolutely love and teach my clients to have is a high-ticket offer. There's nothing wrong with having a digital course and making passive income. I've done that for the past 10 years but having that high-ticket program which is a consultation or mentorship program where people are going to get a little more access to you, you are able to charge a lot more. Charge a premium price, and people will pay you for it.

You can charge anywhere from $3,000 all the way up to $30,000 for this I've actually seen people charge $100,000 and people have actually been excited to pay that. Just think about that. Most people barely make 6 figures a year in income from their job. They're capped at around that $40,000 $50,000 a year. But as an internet landlord having a high-ticket program where someone works with you for let's say 3 or 6 months. You could even have the client meet you in person at your office or you include that in some type of mastermind at a private location. You can charge $5,000 to $10,000 easy and bring in 4, 5 people and you'll hit that income in 30-60 days.

That's the reason why I love high ticket offers and also having that additional access to you, being able to give them more insight. Typically, what happens as well is you're able to get these people results a lot faster. And they will love you more and praise you more and bring you more clients as long as that program is great. The best thing about it is that you can even create a high-ticket program where you're not even the person that is specifically coaching them. You can have other coaches or people that have been through your training coach them. You can set up where it's even a group mentorship and you don't even have to talk with people one on one.

That's absolutely why I love a high-ticket and it's how I was able to scale past a million in revenue by adding that additional program. Now, you may be thinking, well, why would somebody pay me this amount of money, and where would they even get the money from? Well, the one thing that I also teach my clients is that there are different finance and funding programs that are built specifically for coaches that you can use to offer your potential clients to get so they can pay you. You'll make the money upfront and they'll pay a small monthly fee to have those funds to get into the program.

So, think about it just like college. Many colleges offer financial aid. Well, this is kind of like financial aid, but for different people that want to get into mentorship programs. The cool thing is there's no prepayment penalty and it's stretched out for a long period of time. So it's not a big monthly payment.

Let's talk about offers. One of my real estate mentorship programs that we offer clients still to this day is an opportunity to work closely with me for 6 months. Now, in this offer, what we do is grant give them access to our text messaging software. We give them a credit of $500 every single month. We also give them 2,000 skip trace leads as well as access to all of the courses that I've ever made. We build out their lead management system in Podio and they get access to come to our weekly meetings, every single Wednesday that we hold as well as every Thursday are accountability calls.

There's a lot of value that's wrapped around that for that 6-month span. They get access to Me and they also get assigned a coach that's going to help them specifically through the process. As you can see, this offer has a lot that is in it to make it very valuable and the cost of that is $10,000. Now, we've had over 67 people to this day pay us that $10,000. So, you do the math of how much money we've been able to generate, and this is what you can do when you create a high ticket offer that is very valuable.

HOW TO TEACH

One of the best things about creating online courses is that when you do create the content for the course, typically you do it once and you can get paid forever with that same content. Now, depending on your industry, of course things may shift and change, and you may need to update the content every now and then. But for the most part, once you create it it's done and you can sell it over and over and over again. In my premier real estate course, I typically will update it once a year, but most of the content is still relevant. So, there's not a lot of updating that I have to do to it. Now, let's get into how to teach. What you want to do is you want to look at the problem that someone is facing, or what is it that someone is looking to gain.

You see, if you are teaching how to get over a relationship, then the problem is someone going through guilt and anger. You have to look at how do you eliminate that, this will come through various conversations of healing. You're going to have to focus on delivering content that will help them through that. You want to look at it as we already know the end goal of what someone's looking to accomplish, but what is everything in between that has to get done for that to happen?

Now, you want to look at, from a beginner stage of where somebody is, if they don't know anything that has to do with that particular topic or niche, you see a lot of times we are so advanced in our niche and our topic that we forget, the basic stuff that someone does not know. So you wanna start there. If you do not put those beginner things, things in there, you will leave a lot of people that are uneducated in that topic or niche confused and missing those parts that they absolutely need. A prime example in my real estate course, I always talk about the importance of getting an LLC, and why it's a good thing to have but you don't need it.

I explain how to go out there and actually become incorporated as an LLC. Now, some people, already have a company, they already understand the benefits of it, but a lot of people don't. And so that's the reason why I incorporate that. And in my courses, another thing that you probably would want to add into your course, typically, no matter what niche you're in is some type of mindset training. Now, I'm not talking about getting all Les brown or Tony Robbins per se, but sometimes it takes time for you to give someone a shift in their mindset in order for them to prepare themselves for what is coming for them, what challenges and things that they have to prepare themselves, to be able to get through in order to be successful in this venture that they're going through with your own online course. Now, how do we go out and teach these things?

There are various ways. One of the ways that we teach our online course is through a whiteboard or a flip chart. This allows for the customer to connect with me, seeing on camera, but also I get to teach and break certain things down visually so that person can see. Sometimes it's just me writing objects for someone to understand exactly what I'm trying to teach. Sometimes, I might just write out bullet points and then cover the bullet points in detail on camera. Another strategy that we use to teach is mapping out everything in a PowerPoint or Keynote presentation. We will have images on there and words on the screen, and sometimes even diagrams. This is perfect for the person that is a little bit nervous and scared about putting their face on camera. Listen, I understand but I'm be honest with you.

At some point, you're going to have to get past that fear, but for the time being, you can definitely record your content through a PowerPoint or Keynote presentation. Now, another strategy you can do when it comes to teaching is you can just get in front of the camera and talk directly to it. No flip chart, no whiteboard, but literally just talk in front of the camera. I like to do this for our introduction videos. And sometimes, other videos when I'm breaking down stories, it's not the only way you should do a course because a lot of people are visual learners. And so they do need to see some type of examples, or let's say, for instance, if you're teaching someone about rehabbing properties, you might have a cameraman or someone following you walking around and you showing certain different parts of the renovation going on.

So, people can visually see what it is that they need to focus on, on learning. So when it comes to them to have to duplicate that same result, they'll be able to do it. So I mix typically all three of those up. And that's how I put together my course. Now you also which is not my favorite, but you can do audio as well too. If you are talking or teaching someone maybe about how to become a public speaker, well, it may be fit for you to just focus on the audio about how people pronounce certain words, or how they say certain different things. And that can be done typically on just audio. Again, it's not my favorite, but I have created some training that had only audio inside of it. And this is how you're going to go out there and effectively teach. Now, what you wanna do is break things down into an elementary form.

What I mean by that is, there is no need of using the biggest words, trying to sound like you're the smartest person in the room, because honestly your customer is not going to get it. It needs to be broken down to a fifth grade level. Meaning someone in the fifth grade could understand what it is that you're teaching. If not, most people are gonna get overwhelmed, confused, and they're not gonna take any action. And you do not want that to happen with your online course. I almost forgot. But one of my favorite ways to teach is actually recording my screen. Now, I use a software called screen flow for Mac if you have a PC I recommend using Camtasia, and there's actually a free software out there called loom, which you can use on your Google Chrome browser to record your screen. Now, if you are showing certain things that have to do with websites or things that you need to show that are online, your best bet will be recording your screen.

And over it for me in my real estate course, we give away a free text messaging software. And so we have tutorials on how to set up the campaigns and we have to record our screen, because it's not enough to just have those images on a PowerPoint or for me to just talk in front of the camera. Again, you gotta think about your customer. They're visual learners a lot of times. So it's better to be able to show them what you're doing step by step while you're talking them through it. So they can literally copy exactly what you're doing while they're getting that step done.

Now, if you have sold your course, meaning you've pre-sold it before you actually made the content, you need to create the content, but instead of creating it right now, what you can actually do is create it live. And so if you want to go that route, your best bet would be to send a survey out to your buyers, find out from your customers, what exactly they want to learn, or more importantly, what are their struggles. Then what you can do is teach the class, live on zoom weekly. Let's say, for instance, an hour, and a half on zoom every Wednesday for four or five weeks, then you're gonna go ahead and take that content. And that will be put into your online course. As a matter of fact, Desmond who is one of my clients built out his whole entire funnel. He teaches real estate, but a specific strategy in real estate. We took his content from his Facebook lives, and then we put that into his course and that's how he's able to now sell a course that has the content in there. Pre-done is already a great way to be able to profit first, then create the content later.

Now, my suggestion to you once the content is done is get that course out to someone that you know, but someone that is not knowledgeable about that topic, because the thing is you want them to go through the course and figure out are there any loopholes or questions that they may have. Then you can go back and record that content to put in that course, because if someone's a complete newbie and have no idea about the steps, they'll have questions after going through the content and can tell you, hey, what about this? Or how do I do that? And that will help you make your course that much better. Listen at the end of the day, the course is not going to be perfect.

There are gonna be things that you're gonna miss out in the first edition of the course that allows you to go out and add a 2.0 to the course or 3.0 and just continue making it better over time. At the end of the day, don't let that keep you astray of not putting out the content because your advice is needed in the world.

What McDonald's Taught Me About Selling Courses For Maximum Profit

Now, when I was a little kid and I may be showing my age on this. I could never forget the days when we would ride by and see that golden yellow arch sitting high in the air. It was almost like the Batman signal but it was for kids. Kids all across America, all across the world would be so excited riding by seeing McDonald's, because we knew that McDonald's arch meant fun. Fun all across the world.

We knew that not only as a kid that if we were able to get our parents to finally be able to take us to that McDonald's. With the Happy Meal we were also promised a toy inside. And that toy could be all different types of things from action figures to books. You name it. But also, if we were good enough if we were persuasive enough to get our parents to take us inside of that restaurant, we knew that we also could play at the play place. I'm talking about being able to have an area where you can run around, go through slides, and play with those little balls area. Instead of having to pay a fee to play this was all free just by eating at the restaurant.

Every single Saturday, I would beg my mom to take me there because I knew that I would meet other kids, and I would have fun guaranteed, and it didn't cost a dime besides what we spent on the food. Looking back, it was an early sign of what actually compelled me to be able to create offers with my online course that will later on make me millions and millions of dollars. And I'm going to explain to you in this chapter on how you can take some of the same different strategies that

McDonald's used to persuade people into their restaurant, and make maximum profit from the front end to the back end.

So, when you're creating your online course the first thing that you need is a way to bring someone into your world. In the internet marketing world space, we call that a lead magnet. That's leading someone in through magnetic forces that makes them have to give up their contact information in exchange of what you have available. For instance have you ever come across a website that's promising you a free video or a free training or free PDF or whatever? That promise will be held as long as you come into their world by giving your name, email, and sometimes even phone number. That is what we call a lead magnet.

Now, in McDonald's, what they did early on, their lead magnet was a toy. They knew that if we could get the kids to beg their parents to get a happy meal that they would get this free toy. That would get more people coming to their fast-food restaurant to order more cheeseburgers and fries.

They also knew that the Play Place was also a lead magnet once again because they knew that kids were the ones that would beg their parents once again to not just go to the drive-thru, but actually into their restaurant because they would be able to play and meet other kids and have fun.

And boy, did those lead magnets work. I can't tell you how many times I've been able to persuade my parents, my grandmother, grandfather, uncles, and aunts. I would act as if I was hungry even if I really wasn't, just because I wanted to get that free toy or sometimes I just wanted to go in to play at the play place. Heck, sometimes they would even have Ronald McDonald there that is also a reason why kids absolutely love McDonald's as well. Before you go out and sell your course, you have to have that. Like I said, this can come in some form of a free guide a free PDF, like a free checklist. This can be a free training a free video. But it has to be something strong enough where someone going to be willing to give up their contact information to get access to that. So, that's where we have to start off with a lead magnet.

Now, once we've led you into our world now it's up to you to have an offer. Once again that will get someone to pull out their credit card or their debit card and give you money. It's turning a lead into a customer. So, we've talked in past chapters about what the offers look like. And so, once we have the offer down packed now it's time to look at what other things can we upsell to expand how much money we actually bring in on one customer. You see the easiest way to make more money every single time is to get your customer to buy more things from you. It's already hard enough to acquire a customer as it is.

Even somebody being able to give you one dollar of their hard-earned money changes the relationship because they're no longer just a prospect. They're no longer a lead. Now, they are customers and it is easier to sell your customer another product when they've already purchased one of them from you, as long as the experience was good. Now, here's what McDonald's taught me about increasing my Average Order Value which is what we call AOV for short.

You see, Average Order Value is important because this is going to increase your profit margins on every single order that comes in. With McDonald's, they were able to capture this by knowing that when you came in to order a cheeseburger, they knew that you would also be a little bit hungrier but you won't want to get another cheeseburger. I mean imagine going in there and ordering a quarter pounder and then asking you also would you like to buy a Big Mac. Just doesn't make sense. But they knew that something lighter that was still yummy that still taste pretty good was French fries and so they added that as an upsell. They also knew that you would need something to wash that down with. This is why they included some type of soda or iced tea or lemonade as well with it. Boom they patched that up as a value meal.

They also took it a step further back in the day because they knew that maybe some people that were a little bit hungrier, they wouldn't want to order a whole another meal. But they would want more of what they already ordered. That's the reason why they included the supersize me option.

They would literally ask you; "would you like to supersize that" for I don't know, 40, 50 cents more. And most of the time, you would say yes because that included more fries and a bigger drink. This is why McDonald's was able to dominate in the 80s 90s and even now, even though I'm not much of a fan of eating McDonald's. Kids across the world still have that craving of being able to go into McDonald's at least knowing that they're going to get that toy. They have even created monopoly games around their store where you can get an opportunity to win some cool prizes including money. In order to win you have to keep buying meals from them to get the pieces of the monopoly board. And that is why McDonald's still to this day is able to dominate the fast-food market. Because of their average order value is high they are able to create profits year after year.

Now, also, when you're coming out with the course, and here's the key that you want to take from this is that you must have a solution to a future problem that is caused by solving the first problem. When we take it back to McDonald's, they knew that you would be hungry, but you didn't want the same exact thing as a cheeseburger. That's why the French fries are presented. With one of my offers that I have for real estate where we were selling a list of vacant seller leads of people potentially interested in wanting to get rid of their property. We knew that this would create opportunities and deals for our customers but we also knew that in order to make the transaction happen, they needed cash buyers

This is why we presented a list of cash buyers as an upsell on top of the list of the vacant homeowners. Because we knew that this would be a future problem that they would have and this would be the solution to it. And this is the reason why that upsell converted at 40 or 45% any given month. This is what you need for an upsell to convert it has to solve a future problem. You have to make sure that you have conveyed that whatever they bought is solving that first problem, but the good problem that they're going to have is to be next which the upsell is going to cover That is how you make an upsell convert where people are going to be throwing money at you.

Now, also with upsells you can also include a downsell. So, a down sale is saying that let's say, for instance, your customer doesn't have all of the money upfront to make that investment to buy the upsell, but they really do want it. Well, instead of charging them the full one-time price, you could actually make it where they are able to make it to a two-payment price. So, instead of it being a $97 one-time offer, you can make it where it is two-payments of $49, meaning one payment today and another payment 30 days later.

This will also increase your AOV because the downsell will convert when the upsell is not converting as high. Now with an upsell what you want to do is you want to make sure that you convey to them that it's a limited offer. That this pricing for this would never be revealed or shown on the internet ever again. You see when you create that urgency for that offer this is why again, people are going to take you up on it because they know this is a one-time offer. They'll never see it again and it's a great deal and it's also solving the future problem.

Now, in order to also increase your AOV, you can add on to what we call your order form, an order bump. So, your order bump is something that you just bump up into your order by clicking a little check box. Now, order bumps are perfect for including small items anywhere from 15 to $30 or $50 to add-on and this will increase your profit margins dramatically. Because instead of them having to say yes to add something on, they literally all have to do is just check a box. Pretty much a lot of you probably went through this funnel and got this book.

Well, you know that when you ordered the physical book that the order bump that we had available was for you to be able to check that box and add the audio version of this book as well as the digital eBook to be able to get that with your order. A lot of you probably have taken this because it made sense it was very affordable. That is an order bump and how you can use it.

How many upsells should you have? Well, it's really up to you. You can have multiple upsells and multiple downsells. There really isn't any number cap on them. I've seen people have about five upsells to the max. I will tell you probably after 3, your customers probably going to get a little bit upset with you. The good thing about upsells is you don't have to put your credit card information again. It's literally set up where all a person has to do is click a yes if they want it or a no and they click yes, they're automatically charged with their credit card. And that is also why I love having upsells, because it makes the checkout process for your client or customer so dang on smooth.

Create a list of some of the future problems that the person may have. One of the common problems that you can put on almost any course no matter what niche you're in is the fact that they are going at it alone. That they don't have any other people like them whom they can converse with or ask questions when they have something that pops up. That's the importance of having a community. Having an offer where people can join a Facebook group, a discord, or potentially even a monthly or bi-weekly call. This upsell converts like crazy, and it's a upsell once again that can be added to any offer, any niche that you have but people love to be a part of a community and they will pay a price that is recurring where it is a monthly continuity offer something like a Netflix, where they have to pay a monthly fee.

All of those future problems out and this will give you the ideas of what the upsells can be. Again, doesn't have to necessarily be a digital product as well. It could be a service. It could be software. It could be something physical that you even send out or mail out to that client or customer. But think about those future problems. Think about how you can solve them and this is how you're going to create your upsells offer.

Why Leaving Digital Footprints Will Build Trust And Your Bank Account

You see I was born in the 80s, I grew up seeing advertising where it was shown on TV, radio commercials, and that type of advertising was very, very expensive. Just think about running advertising on a Super Bowl having millions and millions of views can cost you hundreds of thousands of dollars just to get those eyeballs. The greatest thing about today is that social media has allowed us to get eyeballs on our products and services for a very, very, very inexpensive cost. I like to say the word investment because a lot of times costing, you never get a return on it. Investing done right you do.

So, leaving digital footprints, will allow the trust to kick in a lot faster. I want you to think about what is the website that everybody goes to look something up. If you guess Google, then you're right. Most people are going to look up your name to see what comes up or if you're more product-driven, they're going to look that product on Google to look for reviews. Now if you just started off new as an Internet Landlord, you may not have many reviews or any at all. You may not have any testimonials or people saying that they've worked with you before. But having this social proof will allow people to see more about you and the thing about it is that people buy from people that they like, know, and trust. So, I'm pretty sure unless you're living under a rock, you have some type of social media.

In fact 9 times out of 10 that's probably how you found out about this book. Now remember what I said before just start off with one to two media platforms. When I say media talking about social media platforms to focus on. Too many people get riled up on should I focus on TikTok? Should I focus on Instagram? Should I focus on Facebook groups? Should I focus on LinkedIn? There are so many platforms that are out there and honestly, all of them work. Just think about it. On all of those platforms, there are either hundreds of millions of viewers and users on their daily or even billions. So, to say that your ideal client or customer is not on there, I doubt it. They are on there waiting. You just have to go out there and put your messaging, and your offer so that people can see what you have available.

So, I'm going to talk about the platforms and what my strategy is, what I give all of my students and clients and you can go from there on choosing which one you will focus on. Right now, I have been focusing on my Instagram account because that has been a way where I can effectively put out daily videos as well as messages on my story to connect with my people. You can post on your Instagram story about your life. You can post about what products and things you have available. And you can post in your newsfeed as well. Just make sure you're consistent on posting. This has helped me to make millions of dollars over the past few years. So, Instagram is something that I'm heavily focused on.

Also, what I like about Instagram is it's very simple for you to grow your following. One of the ways that you can get your messaging out to a lot of people is by going out there and paying other influencers or big Instagram pages to post your content. Instagram accounts like Shade Room or Hollywood Unlocked and many other pages that will allow you to pay them a fee for you to post your content on their page. These prices can range anywhere from as little as $50 all the way up to $3,000. Now obviously the bigger the page the more you're going to have to pay. But listen, don't get it twisted. Some of those smaller pages also work very effectively as well too.

Go look at some Instagram pages. See in their bio if they have some type of contact information. Look at their followers and see their engagement on their post. Look at the comments. Look at the likes. See if these look like your ideal customers, then I would message that page or I would email that page to ask for more information on getting promo. We call this Instagram shoutouts. During the whole pandemic of 2020 From April all the way until August, I paid an influencer page upwards of $6,000 a week just to post me and in that $6,000, I was making 30,000 to 40,000 every single Sunday. Talk about a return on investment. So, that's one of the easiest ways you can go out and grow your page, grow your fan base of customers that are going to want to pay you for your services.

Now, another thing about Instagram is that you can go out and leave what we call digital footprints. Being able to put content out there that lasts for weeks or months, even years where when somebody comes back to look you up, they'll see all the content that you have on the page, they can go through all of the videos, get the value from them, and then go out there and click the link in your bio to go ahead and buy your product or service or book a call to be on your high-ticket program.

Also, what we do is we do a lot of reposting of our content. Because the thing about it is that not everybody is going to see the content that you post on that specific time or day, right. So, you're allowed to go and repurpose that information literally if you want once a month. Just repurposing it on your story, repurposing it on your page and what I mean by repurposing is archiving the post and then reposting it 3, 4 weeks later for your new people to see it. Yes, there'll be some old people that will see the same post again, but the buying cycle sometimes is 6 to 8 times. So, the more they see it, the more they'll connect with it and this will help you to get more people invested in you and build that trust where they're ready to go ahead and buy your product or service.

Lately, I've also been focusing on taking a lot of content that I have on my Instagram page and repurposing that content on TikTok. Why? TikTok has been a platform that has made it very simple to go viral. And the good thing about it is that they pretty much push out content to people based on what they're already into. So, if you're into motorcycles, then your page will be filled with people that are driving motorcycles. If you're into piano you'll see more videos that will be on piano. And that's how people are going viral pretty fast on TikTok. Now yes, there's a lot of dances and things like that on there. But contrary to belief also as of right now the users far as how much time they're spending on the platform.

TikTok has surpassed YouTube far as viewers time. This is amazing shocking but that just lets you know that there are a lot of people on there and yes, your ideal client is on TikTok. That is a platform that I'm focusing on as of right now as well. Now the number one platform to use to get digital footprints and I'm going to explain why is YouTube. You see YouTube can be somewhat like your documentary sitcom in a sense. The reason why I say that is when you post your video content on there, people can watch it over and over again, for years to come. Think about your favorite sitcom shows The Fresh Prince of Bel-Air Martin Seinfeld. You've watched these shows over and over and over again, and some people from back in the day may have not even seen or watch it now. And people from today are probably watching old episodes from back then, and they're getting indoctrinated into those older shows. That is why YouTube is more like a sitcom.

The content that you post on there, it stays forever and it last a lifetime of people being able to go in there, watch that content, and build that trust factor up. Far as being able to go viral or being able to build your page up with a lot of subscribers is a lot of work. You have to be very consistent. You have to post a lot of videos. But to be able to sell your courses and products, you don't have to work focus so much on growing your subscriber base, you're going to be focusing more on having the digital footprints through Google because Google owns YouTube.

So, when someone looks up your products, someone looks up your name, all of those videos are optimized or going to show up on Google and that is the digital footprints that you want out there. When people typically look up my name because I've been in real estate and teaching it for over 10+ years. Those are the things that pop up first. Some of my interviews on a famous podcasts like Fresh and Fit and other podcasts as well will pop up because they have a lot of views. But mostly my real estate teachings, the content that I've put out, those are the ones that are showing up first.

Now, you're going to start to see my content for Internet Landlord a lot more because I'm focusing more on building my other channel up as of right now so being able to build that trust very fast, you're going to want to definitely focus on YouTube and here's my strategy behind it. Post an educational content video once a week you can do 30 videos and shoot them all in one day. And then, what you're going to do you're going to post the content once a week. Now the great thing about YouTube is that you can go out and you can schedule your content to go out on a specific day and time. So just think about this.

You shoot all your videos in one day. You go ahead and get all of them edited made up real nice. You then go ahead and set up your YouTube account weeks in advance, scheduled out for certain days and times, and then boom. They'll be set up again, when people start to come to Google to look up you or your product, they will automatically be sent to all of those videos. They then can just go through and binge-watch the content that you have on there and they are going to be that much more ready to go and buy your products and services.

I can't leave without talking about the Big Elephant in the Room, Facebook. Facebook is not a platform that I focus on as much as I did years prior. However, there are still opportunities for you to leave digital footprints on your Facebook. And in fact, I know some people that that is where their main focus is and they are bringing in tons and tons of leads and sales from their Facebook. So, if you are actively on Facebook more than any other platform then you need to use that for your advantage. Maybe you have a lot of friends on there and you can start to post your content on your feed and generate leads and sales that way.

Another thing is that if you are active in other Facebook groups, it's an opportunity for you to be able to drop some knowledgeable information in someone else's group and get those people to friend you. And then while you're posting content on your own page, you'll be able to lead those people into your lead magnet and get them into your funnel so they can buy your course or your program. I know some people that will create their own Facebook group. And bring people into their world where they're able to show that they are an expert in the specific realm. And they are able to get those people that are in the group to be indoctrinated, lead them into their funnel so that way they can buy their products or services as well too.

It's very time-consuming doing it. I did it before. It definitely was profitable, but I would tell you for as time-wise, if you want to do that, you probably would want to hire somebody to delegate to manage the group. Because it can get overwhelming once your group starts to grow. In fact, I have a group of 14,000 people in my group and I just had to let it go because I just could not manage it. So, Facebook is definitely a place that you can focus your time and energy on, but I would tell you my main focus is to help grow the like and trust of an ideal client or customer.

You're going to want to focus your energy on number one Instagram, number two YouTube. Now number three then I would say TikTok. Then number four Facebook. So, that's the order that I would put my social media platforms or where I would put digital footprints at on those different platforms in that particular order.

Now let's talk a little bit about what the content should be. You see most people think where I don't want to give away a lot of my good content that is in my programs. Because then if somebody goes and sees my free content, they're not going to want to buy my paid content, and that is the farthest from the truth. I want you to have an abundant mindset and understand that the more that you put out there, the more knowledge that you give away free, there is this one thing that will end up happening. More people by law of reciprocity will buy from you.

And what that means is that when people start to see that you are giving away freely a lot of gems, a lot of games, and a lot of information that is very helpful to them naturally. What they're going to do is they're going to feel that they should be spending money with you. That they owe you money. Yes, some of the freebie seekers will take the information and make money from it and go about their way. But a lot of people will feel that they owe you something, because they got and receive so much information, so much knowledge even if they didn't even take the information and do anything with it yet. Just having that paradigm shift in their mindset will want them and force them to want to be a customer of yours.

So, give all your best stuff away for free because the thing about it is, is that even if you gave everything away, people are still going to buy your information because they're going to want to get closer to you. Again, people buy from who they like, know, and trust, and a lot of times, they're buying so that way they can be known by you. Trust me, I've done this with a lot of people that I've invested programs into I wanted to get the connection and so I went ahead and spent the money.

Mix it up and also include a little entertainment. Meaning that it could be educational but also be entertaining as well too. This will show people that you have a personality. If you're a funny person, make sure you showcase that. If you are someone that is very motivational, show that. You want to showcase your personality because people are going to be attracted to you being able to see that you're real. Even if you're someone that is a vulnerable person and you don't mind sharing some of your losses. Do that, especially for women. The women that I see do that are smart, and men you should be following in women's footsteps. They are able to make so much money and get so much of a fan base following them because they are willing to put out there the things that are not going right in their life, and be vulnerable, and that naturally attracts people to them. Because they know that social media will only showcase the best things in life. So, being a little bit vulnerable is showing certain things. It's definitely worth doing.

Now personal relationship stuff. You can keep that away. It's up to you. But showcasing that maybe you had a bad day in business or maybe a contract went wrong or maybe you did a certain mistake on something and it backfired, that's actually good. Because then people get to know that you are real.

With your content, make sure that you are intentional about what you want to happen. We call this a CTA (Call to Action). So, if you're educating someone on your niche and you're giving them a lot of knowledge that they can actually take out and do something with, invite them to come to get more information about your training program. Invite them to get more information on opting in to your lead magnet, or you can go to buying your course or getting on a phone call to be sold to your mentorship program. But you want to do that at the end.

You want to do that after you've got even value and invite them to that call to action. Because this way that the video that you're putting up, the content that you are delivering to them will have a meaning behind it and it will do you such a favor of getting people indoctrinated in and ready for them to go buy your product or service.

When is the time to start leaving digital footprints? The time is now. Even if you don't have your program or course built yet, you can go out there and start putting out the content and building a fan base right now. Now, if you do not have your course built and you would like to hurry up and get things set up. We do have a done-for-you program with our agency where we can go out and build your sales funnel, and your course, and have everything ready to go. So, that way when you do put out this content you will have something to offer people. If you're interested in that, want more information, just make sure to go to "theinternetlandlord.com".

How To Print Money From Emails

How to legally print money from emails. If you're like me, you dread opening your inbox. The thought of having to open up my Gmail account and seeing over hundreds of emails from all different types of advertisers, and people trying to promote their products just gets overwhelming. Emails from staff members, emails from family members sending me pictures, and even notifications from Facebook which I had to turn off because it was just getting ridiculous. Email inbox clutter is real and I think almost every single person goes through it. It is impossible for me to clear up my inbox.

As a matter of fact, I've been thinking about even hiring someone to manage my email because that is how much I dread looking at it. Yet, it's one of the ways that I make the most money in my Internet Landlord business. HubSpot said that 90% of email users check their inbox every single day with some of them checking 20 times a day. I'm pretty sure a lot of you will fall into that same category.

In fact, email generates $42 for every dollar spent on advertising. Giving you around a 4,200% ROI. Making it one of the most effective available options for you to generate revenue. There are four billion daily email users. More than 40% of marketers saw budget cuts to email since the pandemic and nearly 35% of marketers send about 3-5 emails per week. So, why is all of this information pertinent for you? The thing about it is that email marketing is still one of the best ways to generate and turn your prospect into a customer.

You see most people will opt-in for your lead magnet, which we talked about previously. They take some time to get to know you, to get to like you, and trust you. They're willing to go ahead and then spend money with you. On average, in our company we send about 500,000-700,000 emails every single month to our database of over 50,000 people. Now, I will tell you, it took years to build that list up, but I'm going to dive in deep into how you can print money from emails and different campaigns that I've set up have allowed me to generate millions of dollars on the backend.

When people first come into your world. Meaning they're first coming into as a lead magnet. They don't know much about you. The campaign that you want to have set up is what we call an indoctrination campaign. What this would do is it will introduce you, your brand to that prospect, and get them to know a little bit about what you have available. What I like to do is to send an email with pictures of maybe things that I may want to show them like awards that I may have won. I will send content that I have over on YouTube, Instagram, or a podcast for them to listen to or watch. Because again this is building up the trust with someone.

Now, the great thing about indoctrination campaigns is that when you use an email service provider you can set it up where you get all of these emails to send out on auto-pilot. You can have them go out every day or every other day however you want. You can set it up at a certain time, and it's a set it forget it type of thing. That means that when somebody comes in on one day, they'll get a certain amount of emails for lets say 15 or 30 days, then the next person that comes in three days later they'll start at the beginning. And that's why I love the autoresponder of setting up your email campaigns.

Now, what email serve provider should you use? We have used Ontraport for the past I want to say 10 years. However, we've used a lot of other different platforms and a lot of them are good. My recommendation to you is to get ActiveCampaign, it's probably the simplest email service provider to use and if I didn't have Ontraport and was a loyal customer to them, that's probably who I would ended up going with is ActiveCampaign.

Now, the next campaign that you want to have set up outside of indoctrinating people. And let me take a little step back is that when your indoctrination campaign, you want to also include things about yourself. So, giving your backstory of how you even got into this industry or niche. Maybe some case studies on people that you've even helped or some different things and success stories within yourself. Lifestyle you can put in emails about that. That is what you're going to be putting in the indoctrination series and what we do for our client's in our Internet Landlord done for you service we give you 150 emails prewritten out. These templates can be added straight to your email service provider.

Recognition campaign is a bit different. You're not doing a lot of selling. You're more focusing on people getting to know you. But at the bottom of the email when you put little PS, that's a simple area where you can go out and add a link to get more information about your product. Something saying like, 'Hey, if you like this content and you want to hear more about what we have to offer. Go to this link here.' And then you will hyperlink it back to your sales page or your book a call page.

The other campaign that you'll have set up will be one of your lead generation campaigns. This is going to move the prospect from lead to customer. So, you're going to send a various different series of emails. One of them is going to be a lot of benefit-driven of what benefits this potential customer would get once they sign up for your product or service. You're going to send out case study emails pertaining to that product or service to get people in to buy your product. Also, what you want to do is include frequently asked questions, FAQs. Because the quicker you understand the objections or the questions that people are going to have before they purchase your course, you want to go ahead and put that in email and message them that upfront. The faster you can clear objections, that's the faster some going to pull out their wallet or purse, and get ready to pay you money for your products.

Now, what you will also set up is a campaign where if people come to your checkout page but they do not check out, you want to have a campaign set up for them to move back to that checkout page. We call this an abandoned cart campaign and that abandoned cart campaign is a series of 3 emails. You include text messages. We'll talk about it a little bit and this will move back to that page. The good thing about having email service providers like ActiveCampaign or Ontraport is you can put a tracking script from your email service provider onto your sales page and checkout pages. So, that way it's tracking the people from your email address that is hitting that page and the ones that aren't. This will allow you to then retarget them via email with an abandoned cart sequence.

This campaign is super important. We have seen our take rates on our products and services have gone up upwards of 35% just on the abandoned cart campaign alone. Because I want you to think about it like this. Just because somebody comes to your page doesn't necessarily mean that they're going to buy, and just because they come to your page and don't buy doesn't necessarily mean they don't want it. If you are a parent and you might happen to be looking on your phone at the product and you're thinking about buying it. All of a sudden, your son comes and bumps you and spills Kool-Aid on the floor. Now, you have to pick up the mess that's on the floor and mop it and you put your phone down and you forget what you were doing. This happens tons and tons of time. Our attention span is at all time low, right. So, that is the reason why we have to have these abandoned cart campaigns to people back to that page so that way they can go ahead and check out and order our products and services.

Now, another campaign you're going to want to have set up is your re-engagement campaign. Ever so often, you will have people that will opt into your lead magnet and they'll just fall off. They won't open your emails, they won't open texts, and they won't do anything. But they'll still be shown as a contact in your database. Now email service providers really don't like this because there's not any activity going on. They're just holding up dead space. But again, that doesn't mean that they're not interested all the way, maybe, it got lost in the cracks of all their other emails and it just been able to pay attention to it.

So, the re-engagement campaign will be set for after a specific time typically 90 days. They will re-engage with these contact to get them to come back. So, it'll be a series of emails that just get them to click a link just to open the email. Something like, "Hey, are you still there?" Just to get them to re-engage with our emails. And that way we'll put them back into another campaign where we'll be able to continue messaging.

Now, you will also have a segmentation campaign is what I highly recommend and what that is, is you're going to segment people based on certain interests that they have. Maybe, you are selling a product in real estate and people are more interested in learning how to find cash buyers than finding motivated sellers. You can tag people with your email service provider based on the emails that you send out and the ones that they click on, and then from there, you can follow up with them and segment them based on their activity of what they're paying attention to more so and what they're clicking on. This also allows you to send out other promotional advertising campaigns or products or services that you may have. So, that way you can promote affiliate products or other things that you have in your arsenal for that potential customer.

Now, one of the campaigns that I absolutely love, and I typically use this when I want to make some quick cash, especially if I'm going on vacation. I remember in 2016 when I was planning to head to Thailand for a month. The cost of the trip was $4,000 to attend this mastermind on top of the plane and everything. I know I needed some extra money to be over there for a whole month. So, what I did was I put together a campaign that we call a flash sale.

Now, flash sale campaigns are very good because you can slash your product or service in half or even if you cut it by 25, to 35%. Heck, you can even do more than 50%. And what this will do, is it will get the non-buyers that are on your list to take action to buy your products or services because they love discounts. You'll make it urgent that they have to take action on this deal because it's only going to be around for a certain period of time. I've literally seen people do campaigns like this for 24 hours. I've even seen somebody do it for 24 minutes. Typically, you do it for three days, because this will allow you to send out 3 emails, and 3 different texts, and on the last day, you can actually send out 4-to 5 emails or texts that day. Because that's when you're going to shut down the campaign and it forces people to make a decision on buying. A rush of sales will happen on that last hour before the sale ends. We call those buyers deadline dancers.

These are all of the campaigns that we've used in the past 10+ years that made me millions and millions of dollars. And you just want to understand. Not everybody is going to be ready to buy right as soon as you present the offer. Some people need a little bit more trust and more content from you. Just think about it like this. If you're dating and you go out on a date with a person for the first time, typically, you're not going to go and spend the night with them that same night. You're going to want to get to know that person. You're going to want to go on some more dates. You're not going to say, let me marry you on the first date either. It's going to take more time. It's the same thing with your products and services as an internet landlord.

We've had people that have opted in to the funnels that have not paid us for a year and a half, two years later. Why are they taking that long? I'm not sure. But we also have people that come in and they spend money with us the same day. Regardless of the fact, you still have to have these email follow-ups and these email campaigns ready to go because they will produce tons and tons of cash for you.

Now, one of the last things I want to touch on is the power of SMS messages. Yes, text messages is seeing a super increase over the past couple of years. Yes, open email rates are decreasing a little bit but text messages rates open are increasing a lot. One thing most people do not ever forget to open is a text message.

So, on your lead magnet, what you do want to do is include an optional field where someone can leave their cellphone number and opt-in on the form because this will allow you to then go out and text message follow with them as well. We have seen conversion rates upwards of 56% with text messages and we also have 30% of the revenue that we generate from text message follow-ups. So, having this on there is also super key when it comes to being able to follow up and print money from your follow-ups.

So, make sure that you have all of these things in place if you want to be able to legally print money. Just imagine being able to wake up and say I need to pay this bill off. So let me create some value or let me create a flash sale and you send that email out and you generate hundreds or even thousands of dollars. It's amazing. And the feeling of that as an Internet Landlord is one of those things that you feel complete freedom knowing that you can generate revenue from anywhere as long as you have a computer or laptop with an internet connection.

Get Them Off The Fence

Now there have been recent studies that have shown it takes about six to eight contacts before someone makes a move or decision on buying your product or service. And this very much relates to a lot of different things when it comes to life in like we mentioned earlier with dating.

A lifelong decision like marriage typically won't happen in the first week. So you meet someone, you have to go on a few dates. You started to realize and see if you really like this person. Then if everything is going well, you'll naturally progress to those next steps, you know, potentially have kids, getting married, those things, right. And that is also with your customer. Now, the good thing about online sales is that you will have people that will jump in for the first time, right? So the first point of contact, everything sounds good. And those are the people that just jump the gun and get to it. Right. But it's a very small percentage of those type of people. I love those people though. They make your job that much easier, but not everybody has that type of buying personality.

So that way you can get them off the fence and get them as a customer. So one of the things that you can do is follow-up emails as I mentioned in the previous chapter. Now, most people don't think about following up with the point of contact because they feel like if they didn't buy well, they probably weren't interested. But if they didn't buy the first time, there could have been all types of reasons why. I want you to think about it like this. Most people nowadays operate everything from their phone and let's say Susan happened to check out your page and saw the product you were offering. Just as she was going to the checkout page she gets a ring from the doorbell. It's a neighbor asking to borrow something. By the time she gets back to her phone she forgot all about her looking at your offer.

She's already excited and moved on to something else. Or maybe someone text her or called her in the midst of her about to buy your course. Our attention span is very short these days. So these things happen which just causes people not to go through with buying your course. Now, you're gonna have to take some people on a date meaning you're gonna have to provide some content to people as well too. But one of the ways that you can continually message someone, the offer you have available, and be providing value can be through emails. And what you want to do is you want to have a different sequence of emails like we talked about that will try to get people back to your sales page to buy your product.

One of the emails will be a more content-based email. You're going to give away a lot of value to this potential customer of all of the things that they're going to get when they buy the course. Now, how do you make it content-rich? You give away something that is very knowledgeable and will help them tremendously. Then you can explain to them how you go in more detail with that in the course, or you can talk about how this is just one nugget of many that you'll earn when you get access to the program. When somebody is able to get an "aha" moment or get that value from an email like that, their minds are going to say, Man I can only imagine what I'll probably learn when I actually get in the course.

That is how you will get people off the fence and into your portal as a customer. Another email that you can send out is social proof. One of the email subject lines will say something like this if I'm giving a testimonial email; Look what these people had to say about me. The curiosity of that subject line will get most people to open it to know because they're seeing that someone was talking about you, and our minds are programmed to always think it's something negative. So, we're gonna at least open that email up which is what we want to happen.

That's where you're gonna have all of your testimonials and it's gonna lead people back to the sales page or the checkout page for them to buy your course. Now, another email that you wanna send out is something like a frequently asked question because here's the thing. Most people may not be buying your product because they either don't know everything that it comes in the course and don't know for sure if it's gonna help them, They might just have a few different questions or objections that they have not got answered. And that's the reason why they haven't made a decision on buying a course. So what you can do is just send out frequently asked questions, FAQ and all of the objections that people typically have about this particular niche you're in cover them in the FAQs. So that way, if they're already thinking about it, you already solve the problem by answering the question. For example in my real estate course, most people don't have much time because they're working full-time jobs to take care of families.

So they wanna know, how long it will take to actually get through the course more importantly, how much time they have to invest to see results? And I explain to them the way that we do it, a strategy we are able to only have to work really about an hour to two hours a day max. They love that. Now another strategy you can do, which I definitely would suggest a lot of you do is putting together a scarcity or urgency type of email. You could do this by either saying that after a certain period of time, you're gonna take maybe one of the bonuses or two of the bonuses away. You can say that you're gonna close enrollment on a certain day. If you do decide to do that, make sure you are really about that. Don't do a fake closing and then tomorrow you're open back up. You could just say the price is going to increase after this day. So that will get the urgency and scarcity in there for people to take action. Most of these people will go ahead and purchase because they don't want that FOMO (fear of missing out) to kick in.

Now, another thing that you can do to get them off the fence is through retargeting on ads, right? So, if you're doing any type of marketing, you should have, and we get into this in another chapter and we talk about marketing, uh, through advertisements. But when you have an ad, on Facebook, TikTok, or YouTube, you should be having pixels set up on your pages.

In these, it will allow you to track the activity that is happening on your websites and match it up with that person on the social media of platforms. Now, what you can do is you can follow these people around in a sense, and basically show them the ads to get back to your sales page. Think about this. Have you ever gone to an Amazon page to buy something or somewhere on Facebook and all of a sudden, you see a dang product that you were looking at just a minute ago?

Now you're like how did this even show up? Or maybe you saw an ad that popped up on your YouTube and you're like they are in your brain. You're trying to figure out how did they do this? Well, that's because it's retargeting. And you can even upload your list of people to a lot of these platforms and retarget them that way as well, too. That's also the cool thing about running advertisements. If you combine all of these and you really put together a strategic plan, this will work to get them off the fence. Because again, if someone sees you over and over and over again, they're gonna be bound to want to do business with you because they keep seeing you. And you're in their face. Think about it like this. If you were to meet a dentist at a birthday party and he gave you his business card and told you if you ever need anything to hit him up. Now, you have any type of problems with your teeth. However two weeks later, or a week and a half later you happen to be driving down the street. Boom you start to get this toothache.

You just so happen to see a billboard of that same dentist that you met at the party, you are gonna be more likely to call that dentist up. And I want you to think about billboards in a sense of you following up with your emails and your ads. As long as you have the right message at the right time, someone will buy. And sometimes it's not the right time for that customer. It's not the right time for that person, but they will buy as long as you continuously follow with them. Right message right time they're in and they will become a buyer. That is how you get them off the fence and get them from a lead to a customer.

You Have An Obligation To Become Rich

Growing up in Detroit, Michigan around the eighties were very different times. This was the epidemic of crack cocaine. And most of the people that I saw that made a lot of money were dealing drugs. My parents and grandparents did a good job of keeping me from the streets. So that way I wouldn't get too caught up in wanting to be a drug dealer, just like everybody else. I mean, come on now, these guys had the glitz, glamor, attention, the jewelry, the women, the money, and the cars. But I knew I wasn't about that life. I didn't want to go down that path. Yes, we saw sports players and entertainers, but they were all on TV. They weren't as accessible as they are now through social media.

So the thought of becoming rich were always in my mind but it didn't see obtainable. I used to watch the lifestyle of the rich and famous and just wondered what it would take to become rich. It seemed like such a farfetched goal. And honestly, back then even for business owners it was a lot. I mean to pay for advertising, you had to either pay expensive prices to get on billboards, or pay to get on radio, or the expensive price to get on TV.

It wasn't as many entrepreneurs or business owners back then. So, I really didn't have that much of an example of what I could do myself and my skill set to actually become rich fast forward. Now, we are in some great times where, because of social media, it has become so much easier for you to create a million-dollar or multimillion-dollar business. Now, I'm not saying that it's gonna be a walk in the park, but because social media, it gives us access to hundreds of thousands of millions of people. If you can access that many people and get them to spend a dollar with you, you're rich, you make a million dollars.

I was trying to figure out around high school what I wanted to do with my life. I had no clue that I would get into becoming an internet landlord teaching others, cause quite frankly I didn't really do that good in school. In fact I didn't like school. I felt like I was always learning things that I would never use in real life. However when I read this book, one thing that stood with me for years was that you should have one hand up to a mentor and one hand down to a mentee.

Now I did enjoy helping others growing up. I never knew anyone would pay me for it though. I just helped people out of the kindness of my heart because I loved to see other people win.

Another book I had read said that as a leader I had an obligation to become rich. Yeah, I always wanted to be rich for selfish reasons but I started to realize I needed to make a lot of money for beyond my selfish reasons. You see the more money that you make, the more money you're able to give to others. That stood with me because for all the reasons that I wanted to be rich, to be able to take care of myself and buy jewelry, and cars and take some vacations. Which is cool but I had a deeper purpose in life. Every person that does make a lot of money and becomes rich including me has had those dreams, and aspirations, you need that because it's motivation. However, what happens to a lot of people that become rich is that when they only do it for selfish reasons, they typically either burn out, or they're still left depressed because they're focusing on things, that they think will make them happy.

You see rich in my mind means not just financially, but it's R.I.C.H (realizing I create happiness). One of the foundations of being able to become rich is being one with yourself, and being happy where you're at even while striving to get to the next level. This is done by abundance. You will never become rich if you have a poverty consciousness. What needs to happen, which we'll talk about a little bit is shifting the identity of how you view money, and how you treat money. This will allow you to grow rich. One of the things that you need to do is map out how many people you would like to help. This could be some of your family members, if you have kids this could be setting up your children to have trust funds, or investments for when you're gone, or even for your grandchildren.

Think about what community you can help. Maybe, you have a church that you go to regularly that you would like to put some money into, or a foundation or something that you believe in. You see it, can't just be selfish ways. The reason why you have an obligation is that when you have something that you're good at you need to share it with the world, and by sharing that you will receive all the gifts of financial abundance. I personally am a believer in God and, a person that does tithe every single week. I haven't missed a week in eight-plus years, every single Wednesday, I go online and I tithe a percentage of my income that I make for that week. I believe in doing that.

God has blessed me with so much financial abundance. It's only right that I also give some of that money away. You see money is energy and it's not bad to store some of it for savings, but you should not be a hoarder of money. When I make money, I also give it away to others. You know, my obligation becoming rich was not only for me, but a big goal which I did in 2021 was also to retire my mom. It's also to be able to provide for my kids a life I never got to have as a kid. Not to say my life was bad at all. It was great in fact, but as parents, we always want to do better than our parents did. I was also able to buy a house cash in 2020 that my aunt and stepmother live in. These are all the things that when I think about how I've been able to achieve financial success, that this what it was all about. Being in a position to help others. I've also been able to employ some of my family members into my business and help others create their own.

At the end of the day your happiness will come in service and helping others. Now don't get me wrong. I felt very happy when I bought my Rolls Royce, but after driving it for so long it was just like I was driving a regular car. You won't see that or understand it until you get it. My first million dollars, I made from sharing my knowledge and advice to others looking to get into real estate investing. And many of you reading this book, your first million dollars will probably come from sharing your advice or knowledge with others as well.

Follow the steps and the strategies in this book, you could be on your way to making that residual income that creates happiness, AKA rich.

Now I want to first and foremost congratulate you for finishing this book. A lot of people will pick up books and never actually even read them. You know how the saying goes? "It's the start that stops most people". So, I want to congratulate you for not letting the start stop you.

Now, the one thing about getting to the end of the book is implementation. Many people will gather knowledge and they will feel that they're empowered because the whole saying knowledge is power. But I don't believe in that. I believe in you actually taking that knowledge and executing and that is when it becomes your power. So, you're probably at one or two lanes in your life. For some of you, you're in that entrepreneur category, where you've been dreaming or even thinking about becoming an entrepreneur and selling your own digital products and making money online, but you haven't pulled the trigger yet. You haven't found out what it is that you want to do or even if you have, you've been sitting in fear that has been keeping you at a standstill

Well, you can continue doing that life, but if you continue doing what you've always done, you're going to continue getting what you always got. It's time to get out of that category. It's time to go ahead and implement everything that you've learned in this book. In fact, if you want to take it a step further, we do have a program where we can actually show you step by step how you can become an internet landlord and take your intellectual assets, the things that you're good at, and turn them into books, courses, and mentorship programs. If that's something that you're interested in all you got to do is go to "www.TheInternetlandlord.com".

Now, the rest of you are probably in that category number 2. You are an entrepreneur. You're making pretty decent money. Probably more money than the average person that makes in the US or whatever country that you're reading this in. However, you still don't feel free. You still don't have that ultimate freedom that you're looking to get to. Maybe, you do need to make more money so that way, you can be able to hire more people and delegate more things out. Or maybe you need to take what it is that you're doing consistently, and then turn that into an education business where you can teach others what you're doing.

I think about a person like Kevin, who came to me, who makes very good money with government contracts. And he's made a fortune over the past two years in doing it, but he had no time to himself. He was at his job working hours and hours and hours as a government contractor. And so, even though he's been able to see 6 and 7 figure contracts, he hasn't had much time to spend with his family, kids, or really enjoy life. So, when we had Kevin on our podcast, he had told me, 'Chris, I want to get with you so I can get my course out there because I really want to show people that they're missing out on the opportunity of being able to get these government contracts.' And I said, 'Sure'.

So, he became my client. We worked together and we mapped out what the course would look like. I actually helped them come up with the name which we called the course Government Cheese. Now, since working with Kevin. He's been able to launch his course, been able to make thousands of dollars. He even was able to speak on stage about his opportunity and now he's getting offers to be on the podcast and other interviews for shows to be able to promote his course now. Now, Kevin is finally getting his freedom and his time back and he's in a better space mentally than he was before he became a client of ours.

So, if that's you, if you want to have similar success, we do have a high-level mastermind and we do have some different services that we offer to speed up your process of getting your online program launched and ready to go. Again, if that's you, I want to make sure you go to "theinternetlandlord.com". What I want to say is that I appreciate you reading this book and I look forward to you being the next Internet Landlord.